A 31-DAY GUIDE
TO PRAYER

P9-APQ-384

ANDREW MURRAY

BARBOUR BOOKS
An Imprint of Barbour Publishing, Inc.

Published by Barbour Books, an imprint of Barbour Publishing, Inc., P. O. Box 719, Uhrichsville, Ohio 44683, www.barbourbooks.com

Member of the
Evangelical Christian
Publishers Association

Printed in the United States of America.
5 4 3 2 1

A 31-DAY GUIDE TO PRAYER

INTRODUCTION

Prayer, in its simplest definition, is talking with God. It can cover the entire range of human experience and emotion, and God is pleased to listen whatever our topic may be. But in His Word, the Bible, God has also provided some very specific instruction for prayer.

The great Christian theologian, Andrew Murray, has created the following thirty-one day guide to prayer, providing timeless guidance that will enable readers to have vital, truly biblical, prayer lives of their own. The indispensable wisdom in the book will lead you to a closer relationship with God and His Son, Jesus Christ.

Read on for a biblical framework for prayer. Put these words into practice, and experience the power of prayer in your world.

DAY ONE

I bow my knees unto the Father. . .
that he would grant you. . .
to be strengthened with might by his Spirit.
EPHESIANS 3:14, 16

Wait for the promise of the Father.
ACTS 1:4

The fuller manifestation of the grace and energy of the blessed Spirit of God, in the removal of all that is contrary to God's revealed will, so that we grieve not the Holy Spirit, but that He may work in mightier power in the church for the exaltation of Christ and the blessing of souls.

God has one promise to and through His exalted Son; our Lord has one gift to His church; the church has one need; all prayer unites in the one petition—the power of the Holy Spirit. Make it your one prayer.

DAY TWO

The Spirit itself maketh intercession for us.
ROMANS 8:26

I will pour [out]*. . .the spirit of. . .supplications.*
ZECHARIAH 12:10

Every child of God has the Holy Spirit in him to pray. God waits to give the Spirit in full measure. Ask for yourself, and all who join, the outpouring of the Spirit of supplication. Ask it for your own prayer circle.

DAY THREE

With all prayer and supplication in the Spirit,
and watching thereunto with all perseverance
and supplication for all saints.
EPHESIANS 6:18

Every member of a body is interested in the welfare of the whole and exists to help and complete the others. Believers are one body and ought to pray, not so much for the welfare of their own church or society, but, first of all, for all saints. This large, unselfish love is the proof that Christ's Spirit and love are teaching them to pray. Pray first for all and then for the believers around you.

DAY FOUR

WHAT TO PRAY:
FOR THE SPIRIT OF HOLINESS

God is the holy One. His people is a holy people. He speaks: I am holy: I am the LORD who makes you holy. Christ prayed: Sanctify them. Make them holy through Thy truth. Paul prayed: "[God] stablish your hearts unblameable in holiness." God of peace, sanctify you wholly!

Pray for all saints—God's holy ones—throughout the church that the Spirit of holiness may rule them. Specially for new converts. For the saints in your own neighborhood or congregation. For any you are specially interested in. Think of their special need, weakness, or sin; and pray that God may make them holy.

DAY FIVE

*Holy Father, keep through thine own name
those whom thou hast given me. . . . I pray not
that thou shouldest take them out of the world,
but that thou shouldest keep them from the evil.
They are not of the world,
even as I am not of the world.*
JOHN 17:11, 15–16

In the last night Christ asked three things for His disciples: that they might be kept as those who are not of the world; that they might be sanctified; that they might be one in love. You cannot do better than pray as Jesus prayed. Ask for God's people that they may be kept separate from the world and its spirit; that they, by the Holy Spirit, may live as those who are not of the world.

DAY SIX

[I pray] that they may be one,
even as we are one: I in them and thou in me. . .
that the world may know that thou hast sent me,
and hast loved them, as thou hast loved me. . . .
That the love wherewith thou hast loved me
may be in them, and I in them.
JOHN 17:22–23, 26

The fruit of the Spirit is love.
GALATIANS 5:22

Believers are one in Christ, as He is one with the Father. The love of God rests on them and can dwell in them. Pray that the power of the Holy Ghost may work this love in believers, that the world may see and know God's love in them. Pray much for this.

DAY SEVEN

*I beseech you. . .that ye strive together with me
in your prayers to God for me.*
ROMANS 15:30

*He will yet deliver us;
ye also helping together by prayer. . .on our behalf.*
2 CORINTHIANS 1:10–11

What a great host of ministers there are in Christ's church. What need they have of prayer. What a power they might be, if they were all clothed with the power of the Holy Ghost. Pray definitely for this; long for it. Think of your own minister, and ask it very specially for him. Connect every thought of the ministry, in your town or neighborhood or the world, with the prayer that all may be filled with the Spirit. Plead for them the promise, "Tarry. . .until ye be endued with power from on high." "Ye shall receive power, after that the Holy Ghost is come upon you."

DAY EIGHT

Ye also helping together by prayer for us,
that for the gift bestowed upon us
by the means of many persons thanks
may be given by many on our behalf.
2 Corinthians 1:11

What multitudes of workers in connection with our churches and missions, our railways and postmen, our soldiers and sailors, our young men and young women, our fallen men and women, our poor and sick. God be praised for this! What could they accomplish if each were living in the fullness of the Holy Spirit! Pray for them; it makes you a partner in their work, and you will praise God each time you hear of blessing anywhere.

DAY NINE

As they ministered to the Lord, and fasted,
the Holy Ghost said,
Separate me Barnabas and Saul. . . .
When they had fasted and prayed, . . .
they sent them away.
So they, being sent forth
by the Holy Ghost,
departed.
ACTS 13:2–4

The evangelization of the world depends first of all upon a revival of prayer. Deeper than the need for men—aye, deep down at the bottom of our spiritless life, is the need for the forgotten secret of prevailing, worldwide prayer.

Pray that our mission work may all be done in this spirit—waiting on God, hearing the voice of the Spirit, sending forth men with fasting and prayer. Pray that in our churches our mission interest and mission work may be in the power of the

Holy Spirit and of prayer. It is a Spirit-filled, praying church that will send out Spirit-filled missionaries, mighty in prayer.

DAY TEN

Ye shall receive power,
after that the Holy Ghost is come upon you:
and ye shall be witnesses unto me. . .
unto the uttermost part of the earth.
ACTS 1:8

What the world needs today is, not only more missionaries, but the outpouring of God's Spirit on everyone whom He has sent out to work for Him in the foreign field.

God always gives His servants power equal to the work He asks of them. Think of the greatness and difficulty of this work—casting out Satan out of his strongholds—and pray that everyone who takes part in it may receive and do all his work in the power of the Holy Ghost. Think of the difficulties of your missionaries, and pray for them.

DAY ELEVEN

WHAT TO PRAY:
FOR MORE LABORERS

Pray ye therefore the Lord of the harvest,
that he will send forth labourers into his harvest.
MATTHEW 9:38

What a remarkable call of the Lord Jesus for help from His disciples in getting the need supplied. What an honor put upon prayer. What a proof that God wants prayer and will hear it.

Pray for laborers, for all students in theological seminaries, training homes, Bible institutes, that they may not go unless He fits them and sends them forth; that our churches may train their students to seek for the sending forth of the Holy Spirit; that all believers may hold themselves ready to be sent forth, or to pray for those who can go.

DAY TWELVE

I will send [the Comforter] *unto you.*
And when he is come,
he will reprove the world of sin.
JOHN 16:7–8

God's one desire, the one object of Christ's being manifested, is to take away sin. The first work of the Spirit on the world is conviction of sin. Without that, no deep or abiding revival, no powerful conversion. Pray for it, that the gospel may be preached in such power of the Spirit, that men may see that they have rejected and crucified Christ and cry out, What shall we do?

Pray most earnestly for a mighty power of conviction of sin wherever the gospel is preached.

DAY THIRTEEN

WHAT TO PRAY:
FOR THE SPIRIT OF BURNING

And it shall come to pass, that he that is left in Zion. . .shall be called holy. . . . When the Lord shall have washed away the filth of the daughters of Zion. . .by the spirit of judgment, and by the spirit of burning.

ISAIAH 4:3–4

A washing by fire! A cleansing by judgment! He that has passed through this shall be called holy. The power of blessing for the world, the power of work and intercession that will avail, depends upon the spiritual state of the church; and that can only rise higher as sin is discovered and put away. Judgment must begin at the house of God. There must be conviction of sin for sanctification. Beseech God to give His Spirit as a spirit of judgment and a spirit of burning—to discover and burn out sin in His people.

DAY FOURTEEN

[That the children] *might not be as their fathers. . .*
a generation that set not their heart aright,
and whose spirit was not stedfast with God.
PSALM 78:8

I will pour my spirit upon thy seed,
and my blessing upon thine offspring.
ISAIAH 44:3

Pray for the rising generation who are to come after us. Think of the young men and young women and children of this age, and pray for all the agencies at work among them; that in associations and societies and unions, in homes and schools, Christ may be honored, and the Holy Spirit get possession of them. Pray for the young of your own neighborhood.

DAY FIFTEEN

WHAT TO PRAY:
For Schools and Colleges

As for me, this is my covenant with them,
saith the LORD; My spirit that is upon thee,
and my words which I have put in thy mouth,
shall not depart out of thy mouth,
nor out of the mouth of thy seed,
nor out of the mouth of thy seed's seed,
saith the LORD, from henceforth and for ever.
ISAIAH 59:21

The future of the church and the world depends, to an extent we little conceive, on the education of the day. The church may be seeking to evangelize the heathen and be giving up her own children to secular and materialistic influences. Pray for schools and colleges, and that the church may realize and fulfil its momentous duty of caring for its children. Pray for godly teachers.

DAY SIXTEEN

WHAT TO PRAY:
FOR THE POWER OF THE HOLY SPIRIT IN OUR SABBATH SCHOOLS

Thus saith the LORD,
Even the captives of the mighty shall be taken away,
and the prey of the terrible shall be delivered:
for I will contend with him that contendeth
with thee, and I will save thy children.
ISAIAH 49:25

Every part of the work of God's church is His work. He must do it. Prayer is the confession that He will, the surrender of ourselves into His hands to let Him work in us and through us. Pray for the hundreds of thousands of Sunday school teachers, that those who know God may be filled with His Spirit. Pray for your own Sunday school. Pray for the salvation of the children.

DAY SEVENTEEN

WHAT TO PRAY:
FOR KINGS AND RULERS

I exhort therefore, that, first of all, supplications,
prayers, intercessions, and giving of thanks,
be made for all men; for kings,
and for all that are in authority;
that we may lead a quiet and peaceable life
in all godliness and honesty.
1 TIMOTHY 2:1–2

What a faith in the power of prayer! A few feeble and despised Christians are to influence the mighty Roman emperors and help in securing peace and quietness. Let us believe that prayer is a power that is taken up by God in His rule of the world. Let us pray for our country and its rulers; for all the rulers of the world; for rulers in cities or districts in which we are interested. When God's people unite in this, they may count upon their prayer effecting in the unseen world more than they know. Let faith hold this fast.

DAY EIGHTEEN

*I exhort therefore, that, first of all,
supplications. . .be made. . .for kings,
and for all that are in authority;
that we may lead a quiet and peaceable life
in all godliness and honesty.
For this is good and acceptable
in the sight of God our Saviour.*
1 TIMOTHY 2:1–3

He maketh wars to cease unto the end of the earth.
PSALM 46:9

What a terrible sight!—the military arma-
ments in which the nations find their pride.
What a terrible thought!—the evil passions that
may at any moment bring on war. And what a
prospect the suffering and desolation that must
come. God can, in answer to the prayer of His
people, give peace. Let us pray for it and for the rule
of righteousness on which alone it can be stablished.

DAY NINETEEN

WHAT TO PRAY:
FOR THE HOLY SPIRIT ON CHRISTENDOM

Having a form of godliness,
but denying the power thereof.
2 TIMOTHY 3:5

Thou hast a name that thou livest, and art dead.
REVELATION 3:1

There are five hundred millions of nominal Christians. The state of the majority is unspeakably awful. Formality, worldliness, ungodliness, rejection of Christ's service, ignorance, and indifference—to what an extent does all this prevail. We pray for the heathen—oh! do let us pray for those bearing Christ's name, many in worse than heathen darkness.

Does not one feel as if one ought to begin to give up his life and to cry day and night to God for souls? In answer to prayer, God gives the power of the Holy Ghost.

DAY TWENTY

WHAT TO PRAY:
FOR GOD'S SPIRIT ON THE HEATHEN

Behold, these shall come from far. . .
and these from the land of Sinim.
ISAIAH 49:12

Princes shall come out of Egypt;
Ethiopia shall soon stretch out her hands unto God.
PSALM 68:31

I the LORD will hasten it in his time.
ISAIAH 60:22

Pray for the heathen who are yet without the Word. Think of China with her three hundred million—a million a month dying without Christ. Think of dark Africa with its two hundred million. Think of thirty million a year going down into the thick darkness. If Christ gave His life for them, will you not do so? You can give yourself up to intercede for them. Just begin if you have never yet begun, with this simple monthly school of intercession. The ten minutes you give will make you feel this is not enough. God's Spirit will draw you on. Persevere, however feeble you are. Ask God to give you some country or tribe to pray for. Can anything be nobler than to do as Christ did? Give your life for the heathen.

DAY TWENTY-ONE

WHAT TO PRAY:
FOR GOD'S SPIRIT ON THE JEWS

I will pour upon the house of David,
and upon the inhabitants of Jerusalem,
the spirit of grace and of supplications:
and they shall look upon me
whom they have pierced.
ZECHARIAH 12:10

Brethren, my heart's desire
and prayer to God for Israel is,
that they might be saved.
ROMANS 10:1

Pray for the Jews. Their return to the God of their fathers stands connected, in a way we cannot tell, with wonderful blessing to the church and with the coming of our Lord Jesus. Let us not think that God has foreordained all this and that we cannot hasten it. In a divine and mysterious way, God has connected His fulfillment of His promise with our prayer. His Spirit's intercession in us is God's forerunner of blessing. Pray for Israel and the work done among them. And pray, too: Amen. Even so, come. Lord Jesus!

DAY TWENTY-TWO

Remember them that are in bonds,
as bound with them; and them which suffer adversity,
as being yourselves also in the body.
HEBREWS 13:3

What a world of suffering we live in! How Jesus sacrificed all and identified Himself with it! Let us in our measure do so, too. The persecuted Stundists and Armenians and Jews, the famine-stricken millions of India, the hidden slavery of Africa, the poverty and wretchedness of our great cities—and so much more: What suffering among those who know God and who know Him not. And then in smaller circles, in ten thousand homes and hearts, what sorrow. In our own neighborhood, how many needing help or comfort. Let us have a heart for, let us think of the suffering. It will stir us to pray, to work, to hope, to love more. And in a way and time we know not, God will hear our prayer.

DAY TWENTY-THREE

I also labour, striving according to his working,
which worketh in me mightily.
COLOSSIANS 1:29

You have your own special work; make it a work
of intercession. Paul labored, striving according to the working of God in him. Remember,
God is not only the Creator, but the great workman, who worketh all in all. You can only do your
work in His strength, by Him working in you
through the Spirit. Intercede much for those among
whom you work, 'til God gives you life for them.

Let us all intercede, too, for each other, for
every worker throughout God's church, however
solitary or unknown.

DAY TWENTY-FOUR

WHAT TO PRAY:

FOR THE SPIRIT ON YOUR OWN CONGREGATION

Beginning at Jerusalem.
LUKE 24:47

Each one of us is connected with some congregation or circle of believers, who are to us the part of Christ's body with which we come into most direct contact. They have a special claim on our intercession. Let it be a settled matter between God and you that you are to labor in prayer on its behalf. Pray for the minister and all leaders or workers in the church. Pray for the believers according to their needs. Pray for conversions. Pray for the power of the Spirit to manifest itself. Band yourself with others to join in secret in definite petitions. Let intercession be a definite work, carried on as systematically as preaching or Sunday school. And pray, expecting an answer.

DAY TWENTY-FIVE

WHAT TO PRAY:
FOR MORE CONVERSIONS

He is able also to save them to the uttermost. . .
seeing he ever liveth to make intercession.
HEBREWS 7:25

We will give ourselves continually to prayer,
and to the ministry of the word. . . .
And the word of God increased;
and the number of the disciples
multiplied. . .greatly.
ACTS 6:4, 7

Christ's power to save, and save completely, depends on His unceasing intercession. The apostles withdrawing themselves from other work to give themselves continually to prayer was followed by the number of the disciples multiplying exceedingly. As we, in one day, give ourselves to intercession, we shall have more and mightier conversions. Let us plead for this. Christ is exalted to give repentance. The church exists with the divine purpose and promise of having conversions. Let us not be ashamed to confess our sin and feebleness and cry to God for more conversions in Christian and heathen lands, of those, too, whom you know and love. Plead for the salvation of sinners.

DAY TWENTY-SIX

WHAT TO PRAY:
FOR THE HOLY SPIRIT ON YOUNG CONVERTS

Peter and John. . .prayed for them,
that they might receive the Holy Ghost:
(For as yet he was fallen upon none of them: only
they were baptized in the name of the Lord Jesus.)
ACTS 8:14–16

Now he which stablisheth us with you in Christ,
and hath anointed us, is God;
who hath also. . .given [us] the earnest
of the Spirit in our hearts.
2 CORINTHIANS 1:21–22

How many new converts who remain feeble; how many who fall into sin; how many who backslide entirely. If we pray for the church, its growth in holiness and devotion to God's service, pray specially for the young converts. How many stand alone, surrounded by temptation; how many have no teaching on the Spirit in them and the power of God to establish them; how many in heathen lands, surrounded by Satan's power. If you pray for the power of the Spirit in the church, pray specially that every young convert may know that he may claim and receive the fullness of the Spirit.

DAY TWENTY-SEVEN

I will bless thee. . .and thou shalt be a blessing. . . .
In thee shall all families of the earth be blessed.
GENESIS 12:2–3

God be merciful unto us, and bless us;
and cause his face to shine upon us. . . .
That thy way may be known upon earth,
thy saving health among all nations.
PSALM 67:1–2

Abraham was only blessed that he might be a blessing to all the earth. Israel prays for blessing, that God may be known among all nations. Every believer, just as much as Abraham, is only blessed that he may carry God's blessing to the world.

Cry to God that His people may know this, that every believer is only to live for the interests of God and His kingdom. If this truth were preached and believed and practiced, what a revolution it would bring in our mission work. What a host of willing intercessors we should have. Plead with God to work it by the Holy Spirit.

DAY TWENTY-EIGHT

The Spirit of truth; whom the world. . .neither
knoweth. . .but ye know him;
for he dwelleth with you, and shall be in you.
JOHN 14:17

Know ye not that your body is the temple
of the Holy Ghost?
1 CORINTHIANS 6:19

The Holy Spirit is the power of God for the salvation of men. He only works as He dwells in the church. He is given to enable believers to live wholly as God would have them live, in the full experience and witness of Him who saves completely. Pray God that every one of His people may know the Holy Spirit! That He in all His fullness is given to them! That they cannot expect to live as their Father would have, without having Him in His fullness, without being filled with Him! Pray that all God's people, even away in churches gathered out of heathendom, may learn to say: I believe in the Holy Ghost.

DAY TWENTY-NINE

WHAT TO PRAY:
FOR THE SPIRIT OF INTERCESSION

I have chosen you, and ordained you,
that ye should go and bring forth fruit. . .that
whatsoever ye shall ask of the Father in my name,
he may give it you.
JOHN 15:16

Hitherto have ye asked nothing in my name. . . .
At that day ye shall ask in my name.
JOHN 16:24, 26

Has not our school of intercession taught us how little we have prayed in the name of Jesus? He promised His disciples: In that day, when the Holy Spirit comes upon you, ye shall ask in My name. Are there not tens of thousands with us mourning the lack of the power of intercession? Let our intercession today be for them and all God's children, that Christ may teach us that the Holy Spirit is in us; and what it is to live in His fullness, and to yield ourselves to His intercession work within us. The church and the world need nothing so much as a mighty Spirit of intercession to bring down the power of God on earth. Pray for the descent from heaven of the Spirit of intercession for a great prayer revival.

DAY THIRTY

Our gospel came not unto you in word only,
but also in power,
and in the Holy Ghost,
and in much assurance.
1 THESSALONIANS 1:5

[Those who] *preached the gospel*
unto you with the Holy Ghost
sent down from heaven.
1 PETER 1:12

What numbers of Bibles are being circulated. What numbers of sermons on the Bible are being preached. What numbers of Bibles are being read in home and school. How little blessing when it comes "in word" only; what divine blessing and power when it comes "in the Holy Ghost," when it is preached "with the Holy Ghost sent forth from heaven." Pray for Bible circulation, and preaching and teaching and reading, that it may all be in the

Holy Ghost, with much prayer. Pray for the power of the Spirit with the Word in your own neighborhood, wherever it is being read or heard. Let every mention of "the Word of God" waken intercession.

DAY THIRTY-ONE

I am the vine, ye are the branches.
JOHN 15:5

That ye should do as I have done to you.
JOHN 13:15

As branches we are to be so like the vine, so entirely identified with it, that all may see that we have the same nature and life and spirit. When we pray for the Spirit, let us not only think of a Spirit of power, but the very disposition and temper of Christ Jesus. Ask and expect nothing less: for yourself and all God's children, cry for it.

FOR LIFE'S TOUGH QUESTIONS, THE BIBLE HAS ANSWERS.

- Concise, Biblical Insight
- Affordable Tools for Churches and Pastors
- Ideal for Both Friendship Evangelism and Personal Spiritual Growth

A 31-Day Guide to Prayer,
Andrew Murray
1-58660-562-3

Change Your World, Jewell Johnson
1-58660-557-7

How to Conquer Anger, Jerold Potter
1-58660-559-3

How to Conquer Fear, Jerold Potter
1-58660-558-5

How to Conquer Unforgiveness, Jerold Potter
1-58660-560-7

How to Conquer Worry, Jerold Potter
1-58660-561-5

Proverbs
1-58660-563-1

When Life Is Cut Short, Ron Jones
1-58660-556-9

Paperback, $1.99, 48 pages each

AVAILABLE WHEREVER BOOKS ARE SOLD